We would like to acknowledge that
the author of this book is

David J. Deane

This information
has just reached us.

FACSIMILE PAGE OF WICLIFFE'S BIBLE.

JOHN WICLIFFE

THE

MORNING STAR OF THE REFORMATION

JOHN WICLIFFE.

John Wicliffe

The Morning Star of the Reformation

Hiding Precious Treasure
for over fifty years

ISBN 1-880960-43-5

Scripture Memory Fellowship International
P. O. Box 411551 • St. Louis, Mo 63141
Phone: 314/569-0244

http://www.scripturememory.com

CONTENTS.

SMF Edition of John Wicliffe

This biography of John Wicliffe is a reproduction of a book which has been out of print for many years. Although he has not been as well known as those Reformers whom God used almost two centuries later in Germany and elsewhere, his faithfulness to the Word of God and his courage in opposing the ecclesiastical powers of thirteenth century England had such an effect on those who followed, that he is often referred to as the "Morning Star of the Reformation." We are reproducing the book just as it was printed many years ago, and we trust that it will be a blessing to many.

God used Wicliffe in an unusual way at a time in Church history when reading of the Bible was considered injurious to the laity. The few rare portions of the Scriptures which had been translated into English were hidden away in the libraries of the convents and other institutions. Wicliffe felt compelled of God to make the whole Bible available for everybody in the language of the English speaking people of his day, "so that every man in the realm might read in the tongue wherein he was born the wonderful works of God."

The value he placed on the Word of God was explained in his treatise titled, "Truth and Meaning of the Scriptures, " in which he wrote, ". . . that all truth is contained in Scripture; that we should admit no conclusion not approved there . . ." Not knowing Greek or Hebrew, he translated the entire New Testament from the Latin Vulgate version of the Bible and supervised the translation of the Old Testament. There was no simple way of making copies of the translated text, but interest in the endeavor grew and he was able to enlist hundreds of expert hands which copied portions of the Scriptures so that within a very short time the Wicliffe English Bible had obtained a wide circulation, and God's Word was made available to the English people.

After his death, the memory of his name was declared infamous by the ecclesiastical powers, but nothing could stop the influence and power of the Scriptures which he had made available in that land, for, as God Himself has said, "*the word of God is not bound*" (2 Tim. 2:9).

N. A. Woychuk
St. Louis, MO
June 1, 2000

JOHN WICLIFFE.

CHAPTER I.

Papal England.

'We wait for light, but behold obscurity ; for brightness, but
we walk in darkness."—Isa. lix. 9.

N the Middle Ages amidst the nations
of Europe, two powers contended for
supremacy—the Pope and the King.
The Pope, as the Vicar of Jesus
Christ, first assumed the title of
Universal Bishop, and afterwards
claimed temporal dominion over all the
monarchs of Christendom. Long and
fierce struggles ensued in consequence of this claim,
and much blood was shed. In some countries the
strife was carried on for centuries, but in England it
was happily terminated at an early period. The
great man to whose wisdom, patriotism, and piety

the nation mainly owes this happy result, was John Wicliffe.

In the early years of the thirteenth century, the kingdom of England became subject to the Pope. A dispute had arisen between King John and the canons of Canterbury concerning the election of an archbishop for that diocese, in place of Hubert, who died in 1205. Both the canons and the king appealed to the Pope, and sent agents to Rome. The pontifical chair was then filled by Innocent III., who, like his predecessor, Gregory VII., was vigorously striving to subordinate the rights and powers of princes to the Papal See, and to take into his own hands all the ecclesiastical appointments of the Christian nations, so that through the bishops and priests he might govern at his will all the kingdoms of Europe.

Innocent annulled both the election of the canons and also that of the king, and caused his own nominee, Cardinal Langton, to be chosen to the see of Canterbury. But, more than this, he claimed the right for the Pontiff of appointing to this seat of dignity for all coming time.

John was enraged when he saw this action taken by the Pope. If he now appoints to the see of Canterbury, the most important dignity in England save the throne, will he not also appoint to the throne itself ? The king protested with many oaths that the papal nominee should never sit in the archiepiscopal chair. He turned the canons of Canterbury out of doors, ordered all the prelates and abbots to leave the kingdom, and bade defiance to Rome. Innocent III.

smote England with interdict. The church-doors were closed, the lights at the altars were extinguished, the bells ceased to be rung, the crosses and images were taken down and laid on the ground, infants were baptised in the church-porch, marriages were celebrated in the churchyard, the dead were buried in ditches or in the open fields. No one durst rejoice, or eat flesh, or shave his beard, or pay any decent attention to his person or apparel. It was meet that only signs of distress, mourning, and woe should be visible throughout a land over which there rested the wrath of the Almighty; for so did the men of those days account the ban of the Pontiff.

King John braved this state of things for two years, when Innocent pronounced sentence of excommunication upon him; absolving his subjects from their allegiance, and offering the crown of England to Philip Augustus, King of France. Philip collected a mighty armament, and prepared to cross the Channel and invade the territories of the excommunicated king.

At this time John was on bad terms with his barons on account of his many vices, and dared not depend upon their support. He saw the danger in which he stood, and, losing what little courage he possessed, determined upon an unconditional surrender to the Pope. He claimed an interview with Pandolf, the papal legate, and, after a short conference, engaged to make full restitution to the clergy for the losses they had suffered. He then "resigned England and Ireland to God, to St. Peter and St.

Paul, and to Pope Innocent and his successors in the apostolic chair, agreeing to hold these dominions as feudatory of the Church of Rome, by the annual payment of a thousand marks; also stipulating that if he or his successors should ever presume to infringe this charter, they should instantly, except upon admonition they repented of their offence, forfeit all right to their dominions."

The transaction was ended by the King of England kneeling before the legate of the Pope, and, taking the crown from his head, offering it to Pandolf, saying, "Here I resign the crown of the realm of England into the Pope's hand, Innocent III., and put me wholly in his mercy and ordinance."

This event occurred on the 15th May, 1213; and never has there been a moment of profounder humiliation for England.

This dastardly conduct on the part of their king aroused the patriotism of the nation. The barons determined that they would never be the slaves of a Pope, and, unsheathing their swords, they vowed to maintain the ancient liberties of England or die in the attempt. On the 15th of June, 1215, they compelled John to sign Magna Charta at Runnymede, and thus in effect to tell Innocent that he revoked his vow of vassalage, and took back the kingdom which he had laid at his feet. The Pope was furious. He issued a bull declaring that he annulled the charter, and proclaiming all its obligations and guarantees void.

From this reign England may date her love of

liberty and dread of popery. At its commencement
the distinction which had existed since the conquest
between Norman and Saxon was broadly marked,
and the Norman baron looked upon his Saxon
neighbour with contempt, his common form of indig-
nant denial being, "Do you take me for an Englishman?" Towards its close there was a drawing
together of the two races, and from their amalgama-
tion was afterwards formed the bold and strong
English people, who, in the fourteenth century,
offered so stout a resistance to the arrogant claims of
the Roman See.

But, while feeling a dread of the papacy, the
people still held to the doctrines of Rome. Enveloped
in ignorance and sunk in social degradation and vice,
they had not the Scriptures to enlighten their path.
The Bible was a sealed book. Freedom of conscience
was denied, and the religion of the country consisted
in outward ceremonials, appealing to the senses but
not influencing the heart. D'Aubigné, the historian
of the Reformation, states, "Magnificent churches
and the marvels of religious art, with ceremonies and
a multitude of prayers and chantings, dazzled the
eyes, charmed the ears, and captivated the senses, but
testified also to the absence of every strong moral and
Christian disposition, and the predominance of world-
liness in the Church. At the same time, the
adoration of images and relics, saints, angels, and
Mary, the mother of God, transporting the real
Mediator from the throne of mercy to the seat of
vengeance, at once indicated and kept up among the

people that ignorance of truth and absence of grace
which characterise popery."

Foxe, the martyrologist, quaintly says, " The people
were taught to worship no other thing but that
which they did see ; and they did see almost nothing
which they did not worship."

The nation groaned under the encroachments and
exactions of the Pontiff. Not content with the
ancient patrimony of Peter's pence, the Pope strove
in various ways to drain the country of its wealth.
The right was claimed of nominating to all the
important benefices of England. Foreign ecclesiastics
were appointed to rich English livings ; and, although
they neither resided in the country nor performed
any duty therein, they received the revenues from
their livings and expended them abroad.

Besides the actual nomination to Church livings
when vacant, the Pope, by what was called a reservation, assumed the power of reserving to himself the
next presentation to any benefice he pleased ; and by
another instrument, which he called a provisor, he
issued an appointment to such benefice beforehand.
The rights of the legal patron were set aside, and
he had either to buy up the Pope's provisor or allow
his nominee to enjoy the benefice.

In the year 1229, a tenth of the movables of
England was demanded, and obtained, to aid the
Pope in carrying on a war in which he was engaged.
A few years later a fifth was exacted.

In 1352 the parliament requested that " remedy
might be had against the Pope's reservations, by

which he received the first-fruits from all ecclesiastical dignities, a greater consumption to the
country than all the king's wars." In another
parliament held in 1376 a protest was made " against
the usurpations of the Pope, as being the cause of all
the plagues, murrains, famines, and poverty of the
land," it being further stated "that the taxes paid
to the Pope do amount to five times as much as
those paid to the king from the whole realm."

The results of these continual imposts were
ruinous to the nation ; learning and the arts were
discouraged, hospitals fell into decay, the churches
became dilapidated, the lands were neglected, and to
the latter circumstance Parliament attributed the
frequent famines and plagues that visited the people.

Monasteries abounded in the country, and begging
friars spread over the land ; these still further tend-
ing to encourage superstition and to impoverish the
people.

The abuses of the papacy did not however go
unchallenged. In 1229 the barons refused a pecuniary
grant solicited by Gregory IX. ; in the reign of Henry
III. Grostête, the pious Bishop of Lincoln, raised his
voice against the corruption and simony of the
Roman See ; the evangelical Bradwardine, early in
the next century, studied the Scriptures and prayed
for the salvation of the Church ; stringent Acts were
passed, with the view of vindicating the majesty of
the law and guarding the property of the nation
and the liberties of the subject against the encroachments of Rome. But it was not until the later years

of the reign of Edward III. that a successful stand
was made against the power of the papacy; and he
who was the honoured instrument in God's hands of
bringing this to pass, and of bringing to light the
Word of Truth, which had so long been hidden from
the people, was—John Wicliffe.

> How precious is the Book Divine,
>   By inspiration given ;
> Bright as a lamp its doctrines shine,
>   To guide our souls to heaven.
>
> This lamp, through all the tedious night
>   Of life shall guide our way ;
> Till we behold the clearer light
>   Of an eternal day.

CHAPTER II.

Early Years and College Life.

"The steps of a good man are ordered by the Lord, and he delighteth in His way."—Ps. xxxvii. 23.

HE exact spot where John Wicliffe was born is unknown. It is generally accepted as having been in the hamlet of Spresswell, close to the river Tees, and situated about half-a-mile from the present village of Wicliffe, near Richmond, in Yorkshire. Spresswell itself and its ancient chapel which were both in existence in the eighteenth century, have passed away; but the parish church of Wicliffe still stands. In this the future reformer was probably baptised.

The manor-house of the village stood not far from the church. In this dwelt, from the time of the conquest until the beginning of the seventeenth century, the representatives of the Wicliffe family; who were lords of the manor and patrons of the rectory. From this ancient family John Wicliffe traced his descent, though, perhaps as a protest against his career, his name does not appear in the records of the house, and his relatives seem to have distinguished themselves, after his death, by their staunch adherence to the papacy.

The date of his birth is, according to the usual tradition, the year 1324; but probably it should be fixed a few years earlier. He was named John, and according to the custom of the age, was called after the place of his residence,—John de Wicliffe, or John of Wicliffe.

His home was situated amidst scenery of great and varied beauty, combining the bold and rugged hills and highlands of the North Riding of Yorkshire, with the soft and charming landscapes of the valley of the Tees; and doubtless the strongly marked characteristics of the people amongst whom he dwelt deeply impressed his boyish mind. Probably the sturdy courage and tenacity of purpose which he evinced in after life may be traced to the influences by which he was surrounded, as he dwelt among the old Anglo-Saxon people of those North Yorkshire dales, and drank in the historical recollections and traditions of men who, through all the changes brought about by the Norman invasion, retained their hold upon that portion of the kingdom.

Of Wicliffe's early years and education very little is recorded. While still young he was destined for the Church. From the parish priest, or at one of the schools for elementary instruction—which at that time were freely scattered over the country, in connection with the cathedral towns and the religious orders—he probably received his first lessons, and became acquainted with Latin, also acquiring a slight knowledge of Grammar, Rhetoric, and Logic, and possibly Music, Arithmetic, Geometry, and Astronomy, as they were then taught.

When about sixteen he was sent to Oxford. At that time this city contained five colleges, or "halls," as they were then called: Merton, Balliol, Exeter, Oriel, and University; and about the date of Wicliffe's arrival, nearly 30,000 students were studying there.

Some uncertainty exists as to which of the colleges he first entered, Lechler, the eminent German biographer, maintaining that it was Balliol, while others claim the honour for Merton. Merton was then the most distinguished for its learning of all the colleges in this country, and ranked next to the famous University of Paris. Two of its scholars, William Occam and Duns Scotus, had shed especial lustre upon it; while Bradwardine, who was closing his career about the time that the young Wicliffe was opening his in Oxford, had been one of its professors.

Bradwardine was one of the greatest mathematicians and astronomers of his day; but besides this he was deeply versed in the truths of Scripture, and as a theologian he became more renowned than he had been as a philosopher. He unfolded to his students the way of life, and warned them against substituting a worship of mere external forms and ceremonies in place of the true worship of the heart. The fame of his lectures filled Europe; and his evangelical views, diffused by his scholars, helped to prepare the way for Wicliffe and others who were to come after him.

Meanwhile the young scholar made rapid progress; a quick apprehension, a penetrating intellect, and a retentive memory enabled him to master the various subjects he undertook, and he speedily became proficient in the learning of those days.

Latin he wrote with fluency; but as Greek was seldom taught at that time and little known, he appears to have gained but a slight knowledge of that language. He devoted much time to logic and to the philosophy of the age, and also studied the canon and civil law with great success. Foxe states "that he was famously reputed for a famous divine, a deep schoolman, and no less expert in all kinds of philosophy." Walden, his bitter enemy, writing to Pope Martin II., says, "that he was wonderfully astonished at his most strong arguments, with the places of authority which he had gathered, and with the vehemency and force of his reasons"; and Knighton, the historian, also an enemy, affirms "his powers of debate to have been almost more than human."

It is as a theologian, however, that Wicliffe merits the gratitude of all succeeding ages. At that time it was not necessary to read the Bible as a preparation for the priesthood. The Bachelors of Theology of the lowest grade held readings in the Word of God; but those of the middle and higher ranks considered it beneath their dignity to expound so elementary a book as the Scriptures. They devoted their attention to the Sentences of Peter Lombard, a scholar of the twelfth century who made a collection of the opinions of the fathers, or to disquisitions upon speculations of their own. "There was no mention," says Foxe, "nor almost any word spoken of Scripture. Instead of Peter and Paul, men occupied their time in studying Aquinas and Scotus, and the Master of Sentences."

But Wicliffe loved the Bible, and by-and-by he became known as the "Gospel Doctor."

In the midst of the grovelling superstitions which then abounded, men were startled by the approach of a terrible pestilence. Appearing first in Tartary, it ravaged various kingdoms of Asia, and then passed onwards to Europe. Italy's beautiful cities were turned into charnel-houses. Crossing the Alps, it entered Northern Europe and soon appeared in England.

In August, 1348, it broke out in Dorchester, and on the 1st of November in the same year it reached London. One hundred thousand of the inhabitants of that city perished. The infected generally expired within a few hours; the strongest failed after the second or third day. The lower animals were attacked, and their decaying carcases covered the fields. Husbandry was suspended, the courts of justice were closed, parliament did not meet; everywhere reigned terror, mourning and death.

This terrible visitation made a deep impression upon Wicliffe. He frequently referred to it in after life. It sounded like the trumpet of the Judgment Day in his heart, and he felt how awful a thing it was to die. His burdened soul found relief in the study of the Scriptures, and the struggles which he underwent gave him a confidence in God and a conception of the importance of eternal things, which prepared him to face even death and the stake.

Shortly after this, in 1356, he produced his first publication—a small treatise entitled "The Last Age of the Church." He was then about thirty-two. In this, while he deplored the gross corruption of the ecclesiastical system, and anticipated the terrible chastisements of the Almighty in consequence, he pointed out the refuge of the devout, saying, "So when we were sinful and the children of wrath, God's Son came out of heaven, and, praying His Father for His enemies, He died for us. Then much rather shall we be saved, now we are made righteous through His blood."

Of the private life of John Wicliffe very little is recorded. From 1345 to 1365 appears to have been a period of quiet work at Oxford. In 1361, we find him master of Balliol College ; and on the 16th of May in the same year he was nominated by his College to the rectorship of Fillingham, a small parish in the county of Lincoln, about ten miles distant from the city of that name.

This appointment did not, however, necessitate his removal from the University. In all probability he continued for all important purposes to reside in Oxford, and continued a member of the academic body of that city, exercising all the powers and privileges belonging to him as such. An entry exists in the Acts of the See of Lincoln, from which it

BALLIOL COLLEGE, OXFORD (ABOUT THE TIME OF WICLIFFE).

appears that Wicliffe applied for and obtained, in
1368, the consent of his Bishop to an absence of two
years from his parish church of Fillingham in order
to devote himself to his studies at Oxford.

Although this portion of the reformer's life has
been called his quiet work at Oxford, it was none the
less important.   As an active member of the govern-
ing body of his College, and also of the whole
University, he acquired and exercised skill as an
administrator; while as a professor he gave disputations and lectures in various philosophical subjects.
As a Bachelor of Theology he gave lectures on the
Bible; and while others were placing it aside as a
book of secondary importance, he held it up as the
final standard of appeal, and drew from it truths of
the greatest importance to himself and of blessing
for his countrymen.

The nomination to the rectorship of Fillingham
obliged Wicliffe to relinquish his appointment as
Master of Balliol; but in 1365 he was appointed by
Simon Islip, the Archbishop of Canterbury, to be
warden of Canterbury Hall, a new college founded
by that primate a short time previously.   The Archbishop, who was an old fellow-student of the reformer,
gave as his reasons for appointing him to this office,
"his practical qualifications of fidelity, circumspection,
and diligence; as well as his learning and estimable
life."

A year after this appointment Islip died, and was
succeeded as primate by Peter Langham, previously
Abbot of Westminster and a private monk.   The

new archbishop arbitrarily displaced Wicliffe from his office and appointed a new head for Canterbury Hall. This being unjust and in direct opposition to the will of the founder of that college, Wicliffe appealed to the Pope. But Laugham had the greater influence at Rome, and after a long delay the Pontiff, in 1370, gave his decision against the reformer.

> Never hasting, never resting,
>   Glad in peace and calm in strife ;
> Quietly thyself preparing
>   To perform thy part in life.
>
> Earnest, hopeful, and unswerving,
>   Weary though thou art and faint,
> Ne'er despair, there's One above thee,
>   Listing ever to thy plaint.

CHAPTER III

The Pope or the King.

" Dread not, neither be afraid of them."— DEUT. i. 29

S yet Wicliffe has appeared before us only as a man of science—a scholar seldom leaving the precincts of Oxford. We are now about to see him step out from the quiet places of the university city and take a leading part in momentous public affairs. The change, although somewhat surprising, does not denote any alteration in him who was the subject of it. Wicliffe had a great mind; he was a man of high mark and possessed a powerful personality. The scholar will now be merged into the patriot, representing in his own person that interpretation of English national feeling which was so conspicuous in the fourteenth century, when crown and people, Norman and Saxon, united, formed a compact body to defend the rights and interests of the kingdom in its external relations, and especially against the Court of Rome.

We have seen how in 1213 King John surrendered the crown of England to Pope Innocent III., and as a sign of his vassalage agreed to pay 1000 marks annually. The oath of fealty was repeated by his son, Henry III., but prudently evaded by succeeding princes; and the tribute was paid, with considerable intermissions, to the close of the minority of Edward III.

Thirty-three years had passed without any payment having been made, and without remonstrance from Rome, when the nation was aroused by the arrival of a letter from Pope Urban V., in 1365, demanding of the English monarch, " the annual payment of a thousand marks, to be transferred to the papal treasury as a feudal acknowledgment for the sovereignty of England and Ireland." In default of such payment the king was admonished " that he would be cited to appear, and to answer for such neglect, in the Court of the Sovereign Pontiff, who had become his civil, no less than his religious superior."

This demand, as unexpected as it was insulting, stirred the nation to its depths. The England of Edward III. was not the England of King John. During the century which had elapsed since Magna Charta was signed, the nation's growth had been marvellously rapid. England had fused Norman and Saxon into one people; she had formed her language, extended her commerce, reformed her laws, and founded seats of learning which had already become renowned; she had fought great battles, **and won brilliant victories; her valour was felt, and her** power feared, by the Continental States; and when this summons to do homage as a vassal of the Pope was heard, the nation hardly knew whether to meet it with indignation or with derision.

The conqueror of Cressy and Poictiers was ill-fitted to become the vassal of a Pope. The bold and daring spirit of Edward III. could ill brook the insulting summons from Rome. He acted, however, with the greatest prudence ; and, summoning his parliament to meet early in the following year, he laid the Pope's letter before it, and bade it take counsel and say what answer should be returned. This parliament assembled in May, 1366.

Having received the Pope's letter, the estates of the realm requested a day to think over the matter; but on the morrow the Lords Spiritual and Temporal, as well as the Commons, met together and unanimously declared against the claims of the Pontiff.

The debate in the parliament was full of importance for England. Wicliffe was present, and, in a tract which was issued shortly afterwards, has preserved a summary of the speeches :—

The first member to rise was a military baron. " The kingdom of England " said he " was won by the sword, and by the sword has it been defended. Let the Pope then gird on his sword and come and try to exact this tribute by force, and I, for one, am ready to resist him."

A second baron rose. " He only," continued he, " is entitled to secular tribute who legitimately exercises secular rule, and is able to give secular protection. The Pope cannot legitimately do either; he is a minister of the Gospel, not a temporal ruler."

" The Pope," said the third speaker, " calls himself the servant of the servants of God. Very well : he can claim recompense only for service done. But where are the services which he renders to this land ? Does he minister to us in spirituals ? Does he help us in temporals ? Does he not rather greedily drain our treasures, and often for the benefit of our enemies ? I give my voice against this tribute."

" On what grounds was this tribute originally demanded ? " asked another. " Was it not for absolving King John, and releasing the kingdom from interdict ? But to bestow spiritual benefits for money is mere simony; it is a piece of ecclesiastical swindling. But if it is as feudal superior of the kingdom that the Pope demands this tribute, why ask a thousand marks ? why not ask the throne, the soil, the people of England ? "

" Pope Urban tells us," urged another member, " that all kingdoms are Christ's, and that he, as His vicar, holds England for Christ; but as the Pope is liable to sin, and may abuse his trust, it appears to me that it were better that we should hold our land directly and alone of Christ."

The last speaker said : " Let us go at once to the root of this matter. King John had no right to give away the kingdom of England without the consent of the nation. That consent was never given. If John gave his subjects to Innocent like so many chattels, Innocent may come and take his property if he can. We, the people of England, had no voice in the matter; we hold the bargain null and void from the beginning."

Thus spake the parliament of Edward III. In bold and pithy language they declared for the King and rejected the Pope. Their decision ran as follows: "Forasmuch as neither King John, nor any other king, could bring his realm and kingdom into such thraldom and subjection but by common assent of parliament, the which was not given, therefore that which he did was against his oath at his coronation, besides many other causes. If, therefore, the Pope should attempt anything against the king by process, or other matters in deed, the king, with all his subjects, should with all their force and power resist the same."

This decision was unanimous. Not a voice was heard in defence of Urban's arrogant demand. From this time the Pope never explicitly claimed temporal jurisdiction over England.

How far did Wicliffe influence the parliament of Edward III. in arriving at this important conclusion? That he had prepared the way for it by his teaching at Oxford seems certain, but that his influence was more immediately exerted in connection with the present decision appears evident from the fact that very shortly afterwards a doctor of theology, a monk, whose name is unknown, challenged Wicliffe, singling him out by name, to refute certain propositions advanced by this monk in defence of the papal claims.

Why specially single out the reformer, unless he had become a marked man in connection with this controversy?

Whether Wicliffe was actually a member of this parliament it is now difficult to decide, but that such was the fact seems probable. Six masters of arts were returned to represent the inferior clergy, and he may have been one of these; or he may have been summoned by the king as a special commissioner on account of his learning and ability. Lechler thinks that the title assumed by Wicliffe in his reply, "The King's Peculiar Clerk," supports the supposition that the king had specially summoned him to parliament.

In the tract which the reformer was called upon to refute, his antagonist first proposed that the Pope, as vicar of Jesus Christ, was the feudal superior of monarchs and the lord paramount of their kingdoms; he then asserted that the sovereignty of England was legally forfeited to the Pope by the failure of the annual tribute, and furthermore, that the clergy, whether considered as individuals or communities, were fairly exempt, both in person and property, from all subjection to the magistrate. The task imposed upon Wicliffe was one full of danger. Nevertheless, he accepted the challenge, and replied to his adversary.

In opening he stated: "But inasmuch as I am the king's peculiar clerk, I the more willingly undertake the office of defending and counselling that the king exercises his just rule in the realm of England, when he refuses tribute to the Roman Pontiff."

After describing himself as a humble and obedient son of the Church, he proposed to affirm nothing that might be reported to her injury or reasonably offend the ears of devout men, and then he stated his grounds of objection to the temporal power of the Pope. These were the natural rights of men, the laws of the realm of England, and the precepts of Scripture. "Already," he said, "a third and more of England is in the hands of the Pope. There cannot be two temporal sovereigns in one country,— either Edward is king or Urban is king. We accept Edward of England, and reject Urban of Rome." Falling back upon the debate in Parliament, he presented a summary of the speeches then made, and thus placing the estates of the realm in the front, and covering himself with the shield of their authority, he showed to all that the question at issue was the affair of the king and the nation, and not a petty quarrel between an unknown monk and an Oxford doctor.

Shortly after this, in 1372, Wicliffe took his degree of Doctor in Divinity,—a distinction more rare in those days than in ours. The circle of his influence was extended, and he began to be regarded as the centre of a new age. A profound teacher, and an eloquent preacher, he demonstrated to the learned during the week what he intended to preach, and on Sunday he preached to the people what he had previously demonstrated. His disputations gave strength to his sermons, and his sermons shed light upon his disputations. He accused the clergy of having banished the Holy Scriptures, and required the re-establishment of their authority in the Church. Loud acclamations crowned these discussions, and the emissaries of Rome trembled when they heard these shouts of applause.

About this time he published his "Exposition of the Decalogue," an explanation of the law contained in the Ten Commandments.

> All unseen, the Master walketh
>   By the toiling servant's side ;
> Comfortable words He talketh,
>   While His hands uphold and guide.
>
> Grief, nor pain, nor any sorrow,
>   Rends thy heart to Him unknown ;
> He to-day, and He to-morrow,
>   Grace sufficient gives His own.

CHAPTER IV.

Wicliffe's Battle with the Mendicant Friars.

"Woe be to the shepherds of Israel that do feed themselves! should not the shepherds feed the flocks?"—EZEK. xxxiv. 2.

THE resistance of Edward III. and his parliament to the papacy without had not suppressed the papacy within. Monasteries abounded. In too many instances they were the abodes of corruption.

While precluded by their vow of poverty from holding any property as individuals, the monks were permitted as corporate bodies to possess themselves of all the wealth they could acquire. Lands, houses, hunting-grounds, and forests; with the tithings of tolls, orchards, fisheries, kine, wool, and cloth, formed the dowry of the monastery. Curious furniture adorned its apartments; dainty apparel clothed its inmates; the choice treasures of the field, the tree, and the river, covered their tables; while soft-paced mules carried them by day, and luxurious couches bore them at night.

35

Their head, the abbot, equalled princes in wealth and surpassed them in pride.

Gross irregularities frequently prevailed, and as early as the end of the twelfth century so many disorders existed that the whole credit of the papal hierarchy was shaken.

Besides the regular clergy and monks, the country was over-run by mendicants, or begging friars; orders instituted early in the thirteenth century. The Franciscans and Dominicans, as these orders were called, after their founders, St. Francis and St. Dominic, professed absolute poverty. They lived by begging.

Clad in gowns of coarse woollen cloth, girded with cord or sash, and provided with capacious pockets, they traversed the land, preaching ridiculous fables, stories from the siege of Troy, &c., to all who were willing to listen, and soliciting alms from the faithful. They were emphatically the soldiers of the Pope, marching through Christendom in two bands, but forming one united army.

The Dominicans were divided into two companies; the one went forward to convert heretics, the other, by the terrible power of the inquisition, to slay them. More rapidly than the older orders did these become corrupt, and only about forty years after their institution, Matthew Paris, a contemporary writer, exclaimed, "It is an awful presage that in 300 years, nay in 400 years and more, the old monastic orders have not so entirely degenerated as these fraternities."

MENDICANT FRIARS.

The Dominicans first entered England in 1321. They speedily multiplied and spread over the kingdom. Forty-three houses belonging to their order were established, and from their black cloak and hood they became popularly known as the " Black Friars."

The Franciscans by pious frauds endeavoured to monopolise the wealth of the country. " Every year," they said, " St. Francis descends from heaven to purgatory and delivers the souls of all those who were buried in the dress of his order." Numbers assumed his garb in consequence.

These friars used to kidnap children and shut them up in monasteries. Their practices at the universities were so bad that Fitzralph—Chancellor of Oxford in 1333, and Archbishop of Armagh in 1347—affirmed before the Pope " that parents seeing their children to be stolen from them in the universities by these friars do refuse therefore to send them to their studies." He also stated that " whereas in my time there were in the University of Oxford 30,000 students, now there are not to be found 6000." Fitzralph made a special journey to Avignon, where the Pope then resided, and urged his complaints against the mendicants in person ; but although they were but too well founded, the Pope took no notice of them, finding the friars indispensable to him, and knowing that they were his most useful agents.

Fitzralph returned to England, and died three years afterwards, in 1360.

Some obscurity exists as to the date when Wicliffe

commenced his attack upon the mendicant friars.
The general opinion may be expressed in the words of
an anonymous writer, whose manuscript is still
extant. He says: "John Wicliffe, the singular
ornament of his time, began at Oxford in the year of
our Lord 1360, in his public lectures, to correct the
abuses of the clergy and their open wickedness,
King Edward III. being living, and continued secure
a most valiant champion of the truth against the
tyrants of Sodom."

Subsequent investigations, however, lead to the
conclusion that the conflict was not entered upon
until a later date, probably as late as the year 1378,
and it continued until the reformer's death. The
evils with which Wicliffe charged the mendicants
were summarised and published in his tract entitled
"Objections to Friars." This was issued about
1382. In it Wicliffe accused them of "holding fifty
heresies and errors, and many more if men would
seek them well out."

Among the fifty heresies and errors laid to their
charge were the following :—

"Friars say that their religion is more perfect
than the religion of Christ, and that it is more
meritorious to give alms to hypocrites, that say
they are holy and needy when they are strong in
body and have overmuch riches, than to give them
to poor feeble, crooked, blind, and bed-ridden men."

"Friars draw children to their private order by
hypocrisy, lying, and stealing."

"Friars, that be called Masters of Divinity, live as

lords and kings, and send out idiots, full of covetousness, to preach, not the Gospel, but chronicles,
fables, and lies; to please the people, and to rob
them."

" Friars deal not faithfully in showing people their
sins, but flatter them and nourish them in sin."

In reference to this Fitzralph declared : " I have
in my diocese of Armagh about 2000 persons who
stand condemned by the censures of the Church
denounced every year against murderers, thieves, and
such-like malefactors, of all which number scarce
fourteen have applied to me, or to my clergy, for
absolution; yet they all receive the sacraments, as
others do, because they are absolved, or pretend to
be absolved, by friars."

Wicliffe continued :—

" Friars praise more their rotten habit than the
body of the Lord Jesus Christ; for they teach lords
and ladies that if they die in the habit of St. Francis
they shall never go to hell."

He also accused them of making the land lawless,
of being Iscariot's children, betraying the truth of the
Gospel for money, of maintaining that Holy Scripture is false, of exalting themselves above Christ, of
being guilty of simony, and of cruelly persecuting, even
unto death, those who, not of their order, travelled
the country sowing God's Word among the people.

Besides these charges, he held them up to reproba-
tion, declaring :—

" Friars are most perilous enemies of the Church
and of the land; they hinder curates of their offices

and spend needlessly 60,000 marks a-year which they rob the poor people of." And again : " Friars build many churches, and costly waste-houses, and cloisters, as it were castles, and that without need, whereby parish churches and common ways have been impaired and in some cases undone."

While laying bare the vices of the mendicants, Wicliffe also preached the Gospel to his countrymen. The friars claimed, in the name of the Pope, to grant men pardon for their sins. The fallacy of this claim he exposed, but, at the same time, he pointed them to Him who alone could grant pardon for sin. " There cometh," said he, " no pardon but of God. There is no greater heresy than for a man to believe that he is absolved from his sins if he give money, or if a priest lay his hand upon his head and say that he absolveth thee ; for thou must be sorrowful in thy heart and make amends to God, else God absolveth thee not."

" May God of His infinite mercy," said he, " destroy the pride, covetousness, hypocrisy, and heresy of this feigned pardoning, and make men busy to keep His commandments, and to set fully their trust in Jesus Christ."

In thus opposing the begging friars, the reformer ran great hazard. Their power was immense. For nearly two centuries the inquisition had been performing its work of torture and destruction on the Continent. During that period its odious business had devolved chiefly upon the orders of St. Dominic and St. Francis, and these, while appealing to the rack and to the stake as their ultimate weapons of debate, are described as "the confessors, the preachers, and the rulers commonly of all men."

But while the danger was great, the good that resulted from this controversy was also great. The mendicants pleaded the sanction of the Saviour for their begging. "Christ and His apostles," said they, "were mendicants and lived on alms." Men turned to the New Testament to see if it were so, and thus became more deeply acquainted with the Word of God. Wicliffe, especially, was led to a yet closer study of the Bible. The truths of Scripture were revealed to him more and more plainly, and he was led to see how widely the Church of Rome had departed from the Gospel of Christ. The preparation for his great work was nearly complete, and, ere long, the Professor of Oxford will give place to the Reformer of England.

> Shall I, for fear of feeble man,
> The Spirit's course in me restrain ?
> Or, undismayed in deed and word,
> Be a true witness for my Lord ?
>
> My life, my blood, I here present,
> If for Thy truth they may be spent :
> Fulfil Thy sovereign counsel, Lord !
> Thy will be done, Thy name adored !
>
> Give me Thy strength, O God of Power !
> Then let winds blow, or thunders roar,
> Thy faithful witness will I be ;
> 'Tis fixed ; I can do all through Thee.

CHAPTER V.

Wicliffe appointed a Royal Commissioner.

"Them that honour me I will honour."—1 SAM ii. 30.

N this age of liberty it is difficult to imagine the arbitrary power exercised by the Popes of the Middle Ages. In England during the fourteenth century a battle was constantly being carried on between the King and his Parliament on the one side, and the Papal Court on the other.

We have seen how the Parliament in 1366 rejected the demand for the 1000 marks annually, made by Urban V. We have noticed how the country was being drained by the constant exactions of the Roman Pontiffs, and have stated that stringent laws were passed to protect the rights of the Crown and the property of the subject. We have now to witness a continuance of the strife, and to see the measures adopted by the estates of the realm to throw off the yoke which papal tyranny had imposed upon the nation.

Two Acts had been passed; the first, called the Statute of Provisors, in 1350, and the second, the Statute of Præmunire, three years after, especially with the view of checking the papal usurpations.

The first of these statutes declared it illegal to procure any presentation to any benefice from the Court of Rome, or to accept any living otherwise than as the law directed through the chapters and ordinary electors. The second forbade all appeals on questions of property from the English tribunals to the courts at Rome, under pain of confiscation of goods and imprisonment during the King's pleasure.

In spite of these enactments the Pope continued to reserve to himself certain benefices in England, generally the more wealthy livings, and not only appointed to the same, but by his provisor issued his appointment beforehand. The rights of the Crown, or of the lawful patron, were set aside, and the real presentee had either to buy up the provisor or allow the Pope's nominee, often a foreigner, to enjoy the benefice.

In this way the best livings in England were held by Italians, Frenchmen and other foreigners; some of them being mere boys, ignorant not only of the English language but even of Latin; who never so much as saw their churches, but committed the care of them to such as they could get to serve them the cheapest, and received the revenues at Rome or elsewhere, remitted to them by their proctors to whom they let their tithes.

These grievances were felt to be intolerable. The

Parliament addressed a new remonstrance to the King, setting forth the unbearable nature of the oppressions, and praying him to take action in the matter. Edward III., in 1373, appointed four commissioners to proceed to Avignon, where Pope Gregory XI. resided, to lay the complaints of the English people before him, and to request that for the future he would forbear meddling with the reservation of benefices. The ambassadors were courteously received, but they obtained no redress.

The Parliament renewed their complaints, and requested that "remedy be provided against the provisions of the Pope, whereby he reaps the first fruits of ecclesiastical dignities, the treasure of the realm being thereby conveyed away, which they cannot bear."

In 1374 a Royal Commission was issued to inquire into the number of ecclesiastical benefices and dignities, in England, held by aliens, and to estimate their value. It was found that the number of livings in the hands of Italians, Frenchmen, and other foreigners was so great that, says Foxe, "were it all set down, it would fill almost half-a-quire of paper."

The king resolved to make another attempt to settle this matter with the Papal Court. He appointed a new commission, and it is an evidence of the growing influence of Wicliffe that his name stands second on the list of delegates. The commissioners were John Gilbert, Bishop of Bangor; John Wicliffe, Doctor of Theology; John Guter,

Dean of Segovia; Simon Multon; William Burton; Robert Belknap; and John of Kensyngton.

The Pope declined to receive the King's Commissioners at Avignon, and made choice of the city of Bruges in the Netherlands; and thither he sent his nuncios to confer with the English delegates. The negotiations dragged on for two years, the result being a compromise; the Pope engaging on his part to desist from the reservation of benefices, and the King promising on his, no more to confer them by simple royal command.

This arrangement left the power of the Pope over English benefices at least equal to that of the sovereign. The result satisfied no one in England. The truce was seen to be a hollow one, and did not last.

There is reason to suspect that the interests of England were betrayed in this negotiation. The Bishop of Bangor, on whom the embassy chiefly devolved, was immediately on his return home translated to the see of Hereford, and in 1389 to that of St. David's. In both instances his promotion was the result of papal provisors, and looked like a reward for services rendered.

The visit to Bruges was an important one for the reformer. Wicliffe had never before left his native land. The city to which he went was a large and wealthy one, with a population of 200,000. It was the emporium of Europe. Its citizens combined a taste for splendour with a spirit of independence, and evinced a self-confidence and fearlessness which passed with the more patient victims of feudal tyranny for presumption and insolence. At the time of Wicliffe's visit the conference for the settlement of peace between England and France was sitting in Bruges. The Dukes of Anjou and Burgundy, brothers of the sovereign, were delegates on the part of France: while the claims of England were entrusted to the Earl of Salisbury; Sudbury, then Bishop of London; and John of Gaunt, the Duke of Lancaster, son of the King. Wicliffe's position at Bruges secured him access to these ambassadors, and to other persons of note who were then in the city; and his insight into the policy and intrigues of the States and the Church produced no doubt deep impressions upon his mind, not altogether favourable to the papacy and its friends.

He was more than disgusted with the result of the protracted negotiations, and the views which had been opened to him of papal sanctity were such that his rebukes of the corruptions of the Pope and the Papal Court were soon after his return applied with unsparing severity. Avarice, ambition, hypocrisy—these were the gods that were worshipped at the Roman Court; these were the virtues that adorned the Papal Throne.

Soon after his return from Bruges, Wicliffe was appointed to the rectorship of Lutterworth, in Leicestershire. As this preferment came from the King, it may be accepted as a sign of the royal approval of his conduct as a commissioner, and of his growing influence at Court.

Parliament in April, 1376, re-stated the grievances of the country in relation to the papal demands and encroachments. They drew up a Bill of Indictment against the papal usurpations, and set forth the manifold miseries under which the country was groaning through the tyranny of a foreign power which had crept into the kingdom under spiritual pretexts. In this document it was stated that the revenue drawn by the Pope from the realm was five times as much as that which the King received; that the Pope's collector had opened an establishment in London, with a staff of officers, as if it were one of the great courts of the nation, transporting to the Pope twenty thousand marks annually, or more; and that the Pope often imposed a special tax upon the clergy, which he sometimes expended in subsidising the enemies of the country.

They further stated that it would be good to renew all the statutes against provisions from Rome, and requested that no papal collector or proctor should remain in England, upon pain of life and limb; and that no Englishman, on the like pain, should become such collector or proctor, or remain at the Court of Rome.

The nation supported the Parliament, and the statutes against the papal appointments were rigidly enforced. The Pope maintained the strife for a few years, but ultimately had to give way before the firm attitude of the people.

Wicliffe's was the spirit that moved the Commons of England. His graphic style may be recognised in the document of the Parliament; and he it was who once again led the way to victory and to the assertion of the people's rights as the free subjects of an independent realm.

Prior to these events, the Parliament had in 1371 carried a motion imposing a war-tax upon the estates of the clergy, and, in connection with the imposition of this tax, they had made a proposition to the Crown that the King should remove all prelates from the high offices of State, and fill up the vacancies with laymen. Edward III. accepted the proposal, and in February 1372 none but laymen constituted the Privy Council. Among those who resigned their offices in connection with this proposition were William of Wykeham, the famous architect, who was the Lord Chancellor, and the Bishop of Exeter, who was then the Treasurer of the Kingdom.

In the creation of the feeling which brought about this great and beneficial change, Wicliffe was one of the most important factors. His language is definite: "Neither prelates nor doctors, priests nor deacons, should hold secular offices, that is, those of Chancery, Treasury, Privy Seal, and other such secular offices in the Exchequer. Neither be stewards of lands, nor stewards of the hall, nor clerks of the kitchen, nor clerks of accounts; neither be occupied in any secular office in lords' courts, more especially while secular men are sufficient to do such offices."

In another treatise he writes that "prelates and great religious possessioners are so occupied in heart about worldly lordships and with pleas of business, that no habit of devotion, of praying, of thoughtfulness on heavenly things, on the sins of their own hearts, or on those of other men, may be preserved; neither may they be found studying and preaching of the Gospel, nor visiting and comforting of poor men."

> He liveth long who liveth well!
>   All other life is short and vain;
> He liveth longest who can tell
>   Of living most for heavenly gain.
>
> He liveth long who liveth well!
>   All else is being flung away;
> He liveth longest who can tell
>   Of true things truly done each day.

CHAPTER VI.

Persecution.

"Blessed are they which are persecuted for righteousness' sake :
for their's is the kingdom of heaven."—MATT. v. 10.

HE eminent services which Wicliffe
rendered to his country, and the bold
stand that he maintained against the
temporal power of the Pope, caused
him to be held in the highest esteem
by the nation, but brought upon him
the vengeance of the Pontiff and the
papal party.

On the 3rd of February, 1377, at the instance of
Courtenay, Bishop of London, he was cited to appear
on the 19th of the same month, in Our Lady's Chapel
in St. Paul's, to answer for his teaching.

As the day drew near, rumour spread abroad of
what was about to take place, and when the time
arrived a large crowd had assembled at the door of
the cathedral.

Attended by two powerful friends,—John of Gaunt,
the Duke of Lancaster ; and Lord Percy, the Earl
Marshall of England,—Wicliffe appeared at the out-

WICLIFFE APPEARING BEFORE THE PRELATES AT ST. PAUL'S.

side of the assemblage. The Duke of Lancaster and Wicliffe had met at Bruges, and the Duke held the reformer in high esteem, on political if not on religious grounds. He therefore accompanied him, and resolved to show him countenance before the tribunal of the bishops.

The three friends found it a difficult matter to make way through the crowd, which not only lined the approaches to the church, but filled its aisles. In forcing a passage, something like an uproar took place. At last, Wicliffe and his supporters entered the Chapel of Our Lady, where the clerical judges were assembled in their robes and insignia of office.

Lechler thus describes the appearance of the reformer:—" Here stood Wicliffe in the presence of his judges, a meagre form dressed in a long light mantle of black cloth, similar to those worn at this day by doctors, masters, and students in Cambridge and Oxford, with a girdle round the middle; his face, adorned with a long thick beard, showed sharp, bold features, a clear piercing eye, firmly-closed lips, which bespoke decision; his whole appearance full of great earnestness, significance, and character."

The haughty Courtenay watched the movements of Wicliffe and his friends, and beheld with displeasure the humble Rector of Lutterworth accompanied by the two most powerful men in England. Turning to the Earl Marshall he said :—

"Percy, if I had known what masteries you would have kept in this church, I would have stopped you from coming in hither."

" He shall keep such masteries," gruffly said John of Gaunt, " though you say nay."

" Sit down, Wicliffe," said Percy, having but scant reverence for a court which owed its authority to a foreign power—" sit down ; you have many things to answer to, and have need to repose yourself on a soft seat."

" He must and shall stand," said Courtenay, still more irritated ; " it is unreasonable that one on his trial before his ordinary should sit."

"Lord Percy's proposal is but reasonable," exclaimed the Duke of Lancaster ; " and as for you," said he, turning to Bishop Courtenay, " who are grown so arrogant and proud, I will bring down the pride not of you alone, but that of all the prelacy in England."

" Do me all the harm you can," was the Bishop's haughty reply.

" You are insolent, my lord," rejoined the Duke, " You think, no doubt, you can trust on your family, but your relations will have trouble enough to protect themselves."

To this the Bishop replied : " My confidence is not in my parents, nor in any man, but only in God, in whom I trust, and by whose assistance I will be bold to speak the truth."

We quote D'Aubigné for what further took place : " Lancaster, who saw hypocrisy only in these words, turned to one of his attendants and whispered in his ear, but so loud as to be heard by the bystanders, ' I would rather pluck the Bishop by the hair of his head out of his chair, than take this at his hands.'

"Lancaster had hardly uttered these imprudent words before the Bishop's partisans fell upon him and Percy, and even upon Wicliffe, who alone had remained calm. The two noblemen resisted, their friends and servants defended them, the uproar became extreme, and there was no hope of restoring tranquillity. The two lords escaped with difficulty, and the assembly broke up in great confusion.

"On the following day, the Earl Marshal having called upon Parliament to apprehend the disturbers of the public peace, the clerical party uniting with the enemies of Lancaster, filled the streets with their clamour; and while the Duke and the Earl escaped by the Thames, the mob collected before Percy's house, broke down the doors, searched every chamber, and thrust their swords into every dark corner. When they found that he had escaped, the rioters, imagining that he was concealed in Lancaster's palace, rushed to the Savoy, at that time the most magnificent building in the kingdom. They killed a priest who endeavoured to stay them, tore down the ducal arms, and hung them on the gallows like those of a traitor. They would have gone still further if the Bishop had not very opportunely reminded them that they were in Lent.

"As for Wicliffe, he was dismissed with an injunction against preaching his doctrines. But this decision of the priests was not ratified by the people of England. Public opinion declared in favour of the reformer. 'If he is guilty,' said they, 'why is he not punished? If he is innocent, why is he ordered to be silent. If he is the weakest in power he is the strongest in truth !' "

The issues of this affair were favourable to the Reformation. The cause of Wicliffe began to be more widely discussed and better understood by the nation. The designs of his enemies had been thwarted, but their hostility increased. They sent nineteen articles selected from his writings, from his divinity lectures, and from his private conversations, to Rome, to Pope Gregory XI. These articles consisted of statements opposed to the doctrine of the Pope's temporal power, and to the worldly possessions of the hierarchy. They also denied the power of the Pope or the Bishop to excommunicate any man, unless by sin he had first made himself obnoxious to God. They likewise declared that every priest truly ordained was competent to administer every sacrament, and asserted that the highest dignitaries, not excepting the Pontiff himself, might be lawfully corrected by their inferiors and even by laymen.

Speedy condemnation followed the receipt of these articles, and five separate bulls were drafted on the same day, 22nd May, 1377, and despatched to England. Three of these were addressed to the Archbishop of Canterbury and to the Bishop of London, the fourth solicited the aid of the King, and the fifth demanded the prompt obedience of the University of Oxford.

Events happened, however, which caused the publication of these bulls to be delayed. On the 21st June, 1377, Edward III. died and was succeeded by his grandson Richard II., a child eleven years of age. His mother, the dowager Princess of Wales, was a woman of spirit, friendly to the sentiments of Wicliffe.

The first Parliament of the new king assembled in October, two months after his accession to the throne. It was animated by a strong spirit of antagonism to Rome. Wicliffe was summoned to its councils. His influence was growing. The trusted commissioner of princes, the counsellor of Parliaments, he was a power in England. A more opportune moment must be waited for before the bulls against him are made public.

The encroachments of the Pontiffs, and the lightening of the burdens imposed upon the nation through the long-continued war with France, formed the chief subjects of attention in the new Parliament. The complaints against the papal provisions and reservations were renewed, and it was proposed that all foreigners, whether monks or seculars, should leave the kingdom, and their lands and property be applied to war purposes.

The question of the right of the country to retain its treasures, in case of necessity, though the same should be demanded by the Pope under pain of his censures, was also discussed.

The Popes at this time dwelt at Avignon, and were Frenchmen. Their sympathies were with their countrymen in the war then waging between France and England, and part of the wealth drained from the latter country went to help its adversary to carry on the war. Not only was the nation drained of its wealth, but that wealth was turned against the country from which it was taken. This was felt to be unendurable.

The following question was submitted to the judgment of Wicliffe by the Parliament :—" Whether the kingdom of England might not lawfully, in case of necessity, detain and keep back the treasure of the kingdom for its defence, that it be not carried away to foreign and strange nations, the Pope himself demanding and requiring the same, under pain of censure ? "

This question appears, in the light of the nineteenth century, a very·simple one ; but in the fourteenth century the best and bravest of our forefathers were scared by the threat with which the Pope accompanied his demand ; and they dared not refuse it until assured by Wicliffe that it was a matter in which the Pope had no right to command, and one in which they incurred no sin, and no danger, by disobedience.

Wicliffe answered the question in the affirmative. He argued the point on the law of nature and on that of the Bible. God, he said, had given to every society the power of self-preservation ; and any power given by God to any society or nation may be used for the end for which it was given. He thence concluded " that our kingdom may justly detain its treasure for the defence of itself, in every case where necessity shall appear to require it." He also led his countrymen to the same conclusion, by showing that every contribution to the papacy was strictly an alms, and that alms were only properly bestowed

LAMBETH PALACE.

upon the really necessitous. The Papal Court was
rich while England was poor, therefore the wealth of
the country might lawfully be retained.

Furthermore, he challenged the Pope, as the Vicar
of St. Peter, to prove his right to temporal supremacy.
"It may indeed be claimed by you," said he, "in
virtue of some other plea, but assuredly by no right
or title derived from the apostles. For how could an
apostle give unto you that which he did not himself
possess?"

In this manner the reformer led his countrymen
step by step to deny the temporal power of the Pope,
and in doing so to question his right to spiritual
authority. Guided by his counsel, the Parliament
marched onwards, adopting one bold measure after
another. His penetrating genius, his sterling
uprightness, his cool, cautious, yet fearless courage,
made the humble Rector of Lutterworth a most
formidable antagonist, and one whom the Romish
hierarchy saw must not be overlooked.

Meanwhile the papal bulls had reached England.
That addressed to the King found Edward III. in
his grave. That sent to the University received but
a cold welcome, Oxford having too great a regard for
its own fame to extinguish the brightest luminary it
contained. The bull sent to the bishops was, however, hailed with delight, for the adherents of Rome
could not but foresee that Wicliffe's teaching, and the
acts to which it led, tended to the overthrow of the
whole fabric of the Roman power in England.

In these bulls the Pope declared that "information

had been received from persons truly worthy of credit, from which it appeared that John Wicliffe, Rector of Lutterworth, in the diocese of Lincoln, and professor of divinity, with a fearlessness the offspring of a detestable insanity, had ventured to dogmatise and preach in favour of opinions wholly subversive of the Church. For this cause the parties addressed are required to seize the person of the offender, in the name of the Pope ; to commit him to prison ; to obtain complete information as to his tenets ; and transmitting such information to Rome by a trusty messenger, they are to retain the arch-heretic as their prisoner until further instructions should be received concerning him."

Sudbury, who had been advanced to the primacy, summoned Wicliffe to appear before him in April, 1378, to answer for his teaching. The court was to sit in the Archbishop's chapel at Lambeth. The papal commissioners were the Primate and the Bishop of London.

On the day appointed, Wicliffe, unaccompanied by either the Duke of Lancaster or Percy, proceeded to the archiepiscopal palace, situated on the right bank of the Thames, opposite Westminster. A crowd, quite as large, and more friendly to the reformer, than that which besieged the doors of St. Paul's on the occasion of his first appearance, surrounded the palace, and many forced their way into the chapel, proclaiming their attachment to the person and opinions of the Rector of Lutterworth. " Men expected he should be devoured, being brought into the lions' den," remarks Fuller in his "Church History." "The Pope's briefs," said the citizens, "ought to have no effect in the realm without the King's consent. Every man is master in his own house."

While the Primate and his peers were consulting how they might eject or silence the intruders, a messenger entered. It was Sir Lewis Clifford, who had been sent by the queen-mother to forbid the bishops passing sentence upon the reformer.

The threatening aspect of the multitude had produced a feeling of consternation among the bishops; the message brought from the queen-mother caused their dismay to be complete. The proceedings were instantly stopped. "At the wind of a reed shaken," says Walsingham, the historian, describing the scene, "their speech became as soft as oil, to the public loss of their own dignity and the damage of the whole Church. They were struck with such fear that you would think them to be as a man who hears not, or one in whose mouth are no reproofs."

Wicliffe stood the only calm and self-possessed man in all the assembly. A formidable list of charges had been handed to him along with his citation. He handed in a written defence of the tenets imputed to him, introducing his remarks as follows :—"In the first place, I protest publicly, as I have often done, that I resolve with my whole heart, and by the grace of God, to be a sincere Christian; and, while life shall last, to profess and to defend the law of Christ as far as I have power. If through ignorance, or from any other cause, I shall fail in this determination, I ask forgiveness of God, and, retracting the errors, submit with humility to the correction of the Church. And since the notions of children, and of weak persons, concerning what I have taught, are conveyed by others, who are more than children, beyond the seas, even to the Court of Rome, I am willing to commit my opinions to writing. These also I am ready to defend even unto death. In my conclusions I have followed the sacred Scriptures and the holy doctors, both in their meaning and in their modes of expression : this I am willing to show ; but should it be proved that such conclusions are opposed to the faith, I am prepared very willingly to retract them."

He then proceeded to deny that the Popes have any political dominion ; that their spiritual power is absolute, so as to be judged of none but God ; that the Pope has any supremacy over the temporal possessions of the clergy and the religious houses ; that the priest has liberty to enforce temporal demands by spiritual censures ; and he maintained that the power of the priest in absolving or condemning is purely ministerial ; and that absolution will profit no one, unless along with it there comes the pardon of God ; nor will excommunication hurt any one unless by sin he has exposed himself to the anger of the Almighty. Wicliffe laboured hard to show the fallacy of the Pope's binding and loosing powers. It was the belief in his authority to admit to heaven or to consign to the intolerable flames of purgatory that enchained the conscience of the nation. Let this be dispelled, and the emancipation of England will have been achieved.

A second time the reformer returned unhurt and uncondemned from the tribunal of his powerful enemies. A second time he was victorious. The court issued a prohibition against the future teaching of the tenets charged against him; but, as he had given no formal promise to obey it, he continued to declare and spread his doctrines as heretofore.

The subject of the property of the Church engaged much of Wicliffe's attention. About this time we find him proposing to the King and Parliament that there should be a reform of the whole ecclesiastical estate.

The Church was enormously rich. She had, moreover, proclaimed a dogma against that wealth ever being reduced. What was given to the Church was given to God; whoever withdrew any part of the property of the Church robbed God, and committed the awful sin of sacrilege. A curse rested over the man who subtracted a single acre from her domains or a penny from her coffers. Such was the doctrine propounded.

The grievance occasioned was aggravated by the fact that the large possessions of the clergy were exempt from taxes and public burdens. The clergy might, of their own good pleasure, with the sanction of the Pope, grant a voluntary subsidy if the necessities of the State were great; but no taxes might be exacted from them, or contributions laid upon them or their churches.

These riches were the source of innumerable evils. The lands of the Church grew wider, while the area which supported the burdens of the State and furnished the revenues of the Crown grew narrower. The ecclesiastical body became corrupt; pride, luxury, indolence, resulted from this enormous wealth.

To Wicliffe's far-seeing mind the very root of the evil was laid bare. The " goods" of the Church,— her broad acres, her cathedrals and conventual buildings, her tithes and revenues,—were not, he affirmed, in any legal or strict sense the Church's property. She neither bought them, nor won them by service in the field, nor did she receive them as an unconditional gift. The Church was but the administrator of this property, the nation was the real proprietor; and the nation was bound, through its representatives the King and Parliament, to see that the Church devoted this wealth to the objects for which it was given to her, otherwise it might be recalled. The ecclesiastic who became immoral and failed to fulfil the duties of his office, forfeited that office with all its emoluments; and the law which applied to the individual applied also to the whole corporation of the Church.

Such in brief was the teaching of Wicliffe as set forth in his writings.

He not only proposed, but he earnestly pleaded with the King and Parliament that the whole estate of the Church should be reformed in accordance with the principles he had enunciated. Let the Church surrender all her possessions and return to the simplicity of her early days, and let her depend upon the free-will offerings of the people.

This change was to be brought about gradually. He proposed that as benefices fell vacant the new appointments should convey no right to the temporalities, and thus in a short time the whole face of England would be changed.

In making these proposals in the age in which he lived, we see the courageous independence which actuated the reformer, and his fidelity to what he held to be the truth. The Bible, he believed, was with him, and, supported by it, he bravely held and avowed his opinions. His peril was great, for the Pope and all his followers were against him ; but his faith was in Him who is invisible, and in whose hands are the issues of life.

The wealth of the Church, however, remained untouched. Wicliffe was in advance of his age ; and it remained for succeeding generations to recognise the soundness of his views, and to act upon his plan.

> Sow when the tempest lowers,
>   For calmer days may break ;
> And the seed in darkness nourished,
>   A goodly plant may make.
> Watch not the clouds above thee,
>   Let the wild winds round thee sweep ;
> God may the seed-time give thee,
>   But another hand may reap.

CHAPTER VII.

The English Bible.

"The entrance of Thy words giveth light; it giveth understanding unto the simple."—Ps. cxix. 130.

N the 27th of March, 1378, Pope Gregory XI. died. A short time before his
death he returned to Rome, and thus
was terminated the "Babylonish cap-
tivity," as the residence of the Popes
at Avignon has been called by the
Italians.

His successor was elected amidst
the threats and tumult of the Roman populace, who
demanded a Roman for their Pope. The cardinals
elected the Archbishop of Barri, an Italian, who
assumed the name of Urban VI.

By his coarse manners, his injudicious severity,
and his intolerable haughtiness, he alienated the
minds of many from him. The cardinals especially
were estranged, and declaring his election null and
void, being made under intimidation, they withdrew
to Fondi, a city of Naples, and there elected another
Pontiff, who was proclaimed as Clement VII.

Thus was created the famous schism in the papacy which for half-a-century divided and scandalised the papal world.

Urban VI. dwelt in the Vatican at Rome, while Clement VII. installed himself at Avignon. Germany and England, and some of the smaller European States, sided with Urban; and France, Spain, Sicily, Cyprus, and Scotland espoused the cause of Clement.

The effects of this controversy were most disastrous, and are thus stated by Mosheim in his "Ecclesiastical History":—"The distress and calamity of these times were beyond all power of description; for not to insist on the perpetual contentions and wars between the factions of the several Popes, by which multitudes lost their fortunes and lives, all sense of religion was extinguished in most places, and profligacy rose to a most scandalous excess. The clergy, while they vehemently contended which of the reigning Popes was the true successor of Christ, were so excessively corrupt as to be no longer studious to keep up even the appearance of religion or decency; and in consequence of all this, many plain, well-meaning people, who concluded that no one could possibly partake of eternal life unless united with the Vicar of Christ, were overwhelmed with doubt, and were plunged into the deepest distress of mind."

Wicliffe was deeply affected by the events of this papal schism. Soon after its commencement he published his tract entitled "On the Schism of the Popes." In this he adverted to the dispute as having divided the hierarchy against itself, and as presenting a powerful inducement to attempt the destruction of those laws and customs which had served so greatly to corrupt the clergy and to afflict the whole Christian community. "Emperors and kings," he states, "should help in this cause to maintain God's law, to recover the heritage of the Church, and to destroy the foul sins of clerks, saving their persons. Thus should peace be established and simony destroyed."

While the rival Popes were launching their anathemas against each other, Wicliffe, who had retired to his country parish, was sowing by the peaceful waters of the Avon, and in the rural homesteads of Lutterworth, that Divine seed which yields righteousness and peace in this world and eternal life in that which is to come.

Wicliffe was a true pastor. He preached the Gospel to the poor, and ministered by the bedside of the sick and dying, whether freeman or slave. Nearly three hundred of his sermons remain, having escaped the efforts which were persistently put forth to destroy all that issued from his pen. This sufficiently assures us that his labours as a preacher were most abundant.

In his pulpit discourses, as well as in his writings, from this time forward until his death, he frequently alluded to the lust of dominion, the avarice, and the cruelty of the contending Popes, placing these in fearless contrast with the maxims and spirit of Christ and His apostles.

"Simon Magus," he observed, "never laboured more in the work of simony than do these priests. And so God would no longer suffer the fiend to reign in only one such priest; but for the sin which they had done, made division among two, so that men, in Christ's name, may the more easily overcome them both."

Wicliffe's path was onward. He was repelled from the Popes, whom he feared not to speak of as antichrists, but he was drawn closer to the true Head of the Church, the Lord Jesus. The Bible became increasingly precious, and the reformer now issued his work "On the Truth and Meaning of Scripture." In this he maintained the supreme authority of the Word of God, the right of private judgment, and the sufficiency of Christ's law by itself to rule Christ's Church.

The labours which devolved upon him, and the harassing attacks of his foes, were more than his frame could bear. In 1379 he fell dangerously ill at Oxford. Great was the joy in the monasteries; but for that joy to be complete the heretic must recant. Four regents, representing the four orders of friars, accompanied by four aldermen, were deputed to visit their dying enemy. They hastened to his dwelling, and found him stretched upon his bed, calm and serene. "You have death on your lips," said they; "be touched by your faults, and retract in our presence all that you have said to our injury." Wicliffe remained silent, and the monks flattered themselves with an easy victory. But the nearer the reformer approached eternity the greater was his horror of monkery. The consolation he had found in Jesus Christ had given him fresh energy. He begged his servant to raise him on his couch. Then, feeble and pale, and scarcely able to support himself, he turned towards the friars, who were waiting for his recantation, and opening his livid lips, and fixing on them a piercing look, he said with emphasis, " I shall not die, but live, and again declare the evil deeds of the friars." The monks rushed in astonishment and confusion from his chamber.

Wicliffe's prediction was verified, and he lived to complete the most glorious of his works—the translation of the Scriptures into the language of the people.

The Word of God had been banished into a mysterious obscurity. It is true that several attempts had been made to paraphrase or to translate various portions. The venerable Bede translated the Lord's Prayer and the Gospel of St. John into Saxon in the eighth century; the learned men at Alfred's court translated the four evangelists; Elfric, in the reign of Ethelred, translated some books of the Old Testament; an Anglo-Norman priest paraphrased the Gospels and the Acts; Richard Rolle, " the hermit of Hampole," and some pious clerks in the fourteenth century, produced a version of the Psalms, the Gospels, and the Epistles; but these rare volumes were hidden, like theological curiosities, in the libraries of the convents.

In Wicliffe's time, it was a maxim that the reading

WICLIFFE AND THE FRIARS.

of the Bible was injurious to the laity, and accordingly the priests forbade it. Oral tradition alone preserved among the people the histories of the Holy Scriptures, mingled with legends of the saints.

The result of previous labours in furnishing vernacular versions of the Scriptures is thus summed up by Lechler: " A translation of the entire Bible was never during this whole period accomplished in England, and was never even apparently contemplated. The Psalter was the only book which was fully and literally translated into all the three languages, —Anglo-Saxon, Anglo-Norman, and Old English. In addition, several books of Scripture, especially Old Testament books, were translated partially or in select passages—*e.g.*, by Elfric, leaving out of view poetical versions and the Gospel of St. John, translated by Bede, which celebrated work has not come down to us. Last of all—and this fact is of great importance—in none of these translations was it designed to make the Word of God accessible to the mass of the people, and to spread Scriptural knowledge among them. The only object which was had in view was partly to furnish aid to the clergy, and to render a service to the educated class."

Such was the state of Biblical translation when Wicliffe undertook his great work. His idea was to give the whole Bible in the vernacular to the people of England, so that every man in the realm might read in the tongue wherein he was born the wonderful works of God.

The motives which urged him to this enterprise

may be gathered from some of his writings about this time. In his treatise on the " Truth and Meaning of Scripture," he maintained the sufficiency of Christ's law for all purposes of doctrine, discipline, and daily conduct ; and he argued " that a Christian man, well understanding it, may gather sufficient knowledge during his pilgrimage upon earth; that all truth is contained in Scripture ; that we should admit of no conclusion not approved there ; that there is no court beside the Court of Heaven ; that though there were a hundred Popes, and all the friars in the world were turned into cardinals, yet should we learn more from the Gospel than we should from all that multitude; and that true sons will in no wise go about to infringe the will and testament of their Heavenly Father."

Later on he wrote : " As the faith of the Church is contained in the Scriptures, the more these are known in an orthodox sense the better."

A few years only of broken health remained for the accomplishment of his great undertaking; his intellectual vigour, however, was unimpaired. He was ignorant of Greek and Hebrew, but he was a good Latin scholar, and above all he loved the Bible ; he understood it, and he desired to communicate its treasures to others.

While the papal world was in commotion, in his quiet Rectory of Lutterworth he set himself down to his task. With the Latin Vulgate open before him —that book which all his life he had studied—he translated verse after verse, rendering into the English tongue those sublime truths which had ever been to him strength, guidance, and consolation.

The whole of the New Testament was translated by himself; but the Old Testament appears to have been translated, under his direction, by one of his friends—probably being carried on while the New was in progress, and the translation effected by Dr. Nicholas Hereford, of Oxford. It was, however, partly revised by Wicliffe.

The grand work was finished by 1382. As a version of the Scriptures it was remarkably truthful and spirited. Hereford's portion was very literal, keeping close to the Latin text, but the books which Wicliffe translated were kept thoroughly in accordance with the spirit of his mother tongue, and the requirements of English readers; the translation therefore is so simple as to be thoroughly readable.

We give, by way of extract, John xiv. verses 1 to 4, as contained in this version :—

> " Be not youre herte afraied, ne drede it;
> ye bileuen in God, and bileue ye in
> me. In the hous of my fadir ben
> many dwellyngis ; if ony thing lesse,
> Y hadde seid to you, for Y go to make
> redi to you a place. And if Y go, and
> make redi to you a place, eftsoones Y come,
> and Y schal take you to my silf, that
> where Y am, ye be. And whidur Y go,
> ye witen, and ye witen the weie."

The translation ended, the next effort of the reformer was to get the book placed if possible within the reach of all. " When the work of trans-

lating was ended," says Dr. Wylie, in his " History of
Protestantism," " the nearly as difficult work of publishing began. In those days there was no printing-
press to multiply copies by the thousand as in
our times, and no publishing firm to circulate these
thousands over the kingdom. The author himself
had to see to all this. The methods of publishing
a book in that age were various. The more common
way was to place a copy in the hall of some convent
or in the library of some college, where all might
come and read, and, if the book pleased, order a copy
to be made for their own use. . . . Others set up
pulpits at cross ways, and places of public resort, and
read portions of their work in the hearing of the
audiences that gathered round them, and those who
liked what they heard bought copies for themselves.
But Wicliffe did not need to have recourse to any
of these expedients. The interest taken in the man
and in his work, enlisted a hundred expert hands,
who, though they toiled to multiply copies, could
scarcely supply the many who were eager to buy.
Some ordered complete copies to be made for them ;
others were content with portions ; the same copy
served several families in many instances, and in a
very short time Wicliffe's English Bible had obtained
a wide circulation, and brought a new life into many
an English home."

In the work of diffusing the Scriptures his " poor
priests " doubtless assisted.

The importance of preaching deeply impressed the
reformer. " The highest service," said he, " that men

may attain to on earth is to preach the Word of God."
He saw the begging friars strolling over the country,
preaching the legends of saints and the history of the
Trojan war, captivating the people, and he felt the
need of doing for the glory of God what they did to
fill their wallets. Turning to the most pious of his
disciples, he said, "Go and preach, it is the sublimest
work. After your sermon is ended, do you visit the
sick, the aged, the poor, the blind, and the lame, and
succour them according to your ability."

These "poor priests," as they were called, set off
barefoot, a staff in their hands, clothed in a coarse
robe, living on alms, and satisfied with the plainest
food. They stopped in the fields near some village,
in the churchyards, in the market-places of the
towns, and sometimes even in the churches. The
people thronged around, as with a popular eloquence
they urged them to repentance and pointed out the
way of salvation by faith in the Lord Jesus Christ.

One who became widely known, and who in an
especial manner gained the affections of the people,
was named John Ashton. He might frequently have
been seen journeying along the highway engaged in
his Master's service, or standing under some tree by
the roadside preaching to an attentive crowd, or seated
at some lowly cottage hearth telling of the love of
Jesus.

These evangelists travelled throughout the land,
finding favour with the people, but being persecuted
by the Church. In 1382 Knighton, a contemporary
writer, asserted that "their number very much

increased, and that, starting like saplings from the root of a tree, they were multiplied, and filled every place within the compass of the land."

The doctrines of the reformer were thus disseminated over the country, and they became known to all classes of society. Wicliffe afterwards asserted that a third of the priests of England were of his sentiment on the question of the eucharist, and among the common people his disciples were innumerable. "You could not meet two men on the highway," said one of his enemies, "but one of them was a Wicliffite."

As soon as Wicliffe's translation of the Bible began to be scattered abroad, a great outcry was made by the priests and their followers. He had committed a crime unknown to former ages. He was a heretic, a sacrilegious man; he had broken into the temple and stolen the sacred vessels; he had fired the House of God. Knighton, who was canon of Leicester, reflects the spirit of the clergy when he says, adverting to the zeal of Wicliffe in giving the Scriptures to the people: "Christ delivered his Gospel to the clergy and doctors of the Church, that they might administer to the laity and to weaker persons, according to the state of the times and the wants of men. But this Master John Wicliffe translated it out of Latin into English, and thus laid it more open to the laity, and to women who could read, than it had formerly been to the most learned of the clergy, even to those of them who had the best understanding. And in this way the Gospel pearl is cast abroad, and trodden under foot of swine, and that which was before precious to both clergy and laity is rendered, as it were, the common jest of both. The jewel of the Church is turned into the sport of the people, and what was hitherto the principal gift of the clergy and divines is made for ever common to the laity."

Those who love the Word of God look not, however, upon Wicliffe's act as a crime; they rather count his translation of the Scriptures not only as one of the greatest ornaments of the English language of his age, but as being the noblest monument of himself.

> Search the Scriptures for salvation,
>   Christ the Lord has told us so;
> Every tongue and every nation
>   Should the Holy Bible know;
> God's message 'tis, of love and life
> Sent to a world of sin and strife

CHAPTER VIII.

Transubstantiation.

" The words that I speak unto you, they are spirit, and they are life."—JOHN vi. 63.

ICLIFFE'S great work was accomplished, but his labours were not yet over. A brief period must elapse before he shall be called home to receive his reward. He was old and feeble, and needed repose; but the honour of God and the welfare of his country were dear to his heart, and once more he girded himself for the conflict; this time turning to attack the doctrinal system of the Church of Rome.

The doctrine of Transubstantiation, one of the chief supports of the Romish Church, was brought into England by the Norman priests at the time of the Conquest. In this dogma the Church of Rome teaches "that by the sacramental words duly pronounced by the priest, the bread and wine upon the altar are transubstantiated, or substantially converted into the true body and blood of Christ; so that after consecration there is not in that venerable sacrament the material bread and wine which before existed, considered in their own substances or natures, but only the species of the same, under which are contained the true body of Christ, and His blood—not figuratively, but essentially, substantially, and corporally; so that Christ is verily there in His own proper bodily presence."

In the spring of 1381, Wicliffe posted up at Oxford twelve theses, or short propositions, in which he denied the dogma of transubstantiation, and challenged those of a contrary opinion to debate the matter with him. The first of these theses was as follows: "The consecrated host which we see upon the altar is neither Christ nor any part of Christ, but an efficacious sign of him." Wicliffe argued that the bread and wine were as truly bread and wine after as before their consecration.

The publication of these theses caused great commotion at Oxford. At this time the larger portion of the honours of the University was possessed by the religious orders. All shouted heresy, but no one dared to prove it to the author of the objectionable sentences.

A council of twelve—four secular doctors and eight monks—was summoned by William Barton, the Chancellor of the University, and unanimously condemned Wicliffe's opinions as heretical, and threatened heavy penalties against any one who should teach them in the University or listen to the teaching of them there.

Wicliffe was seated in his chair as professor, lect-

uring upon the eucharist to his pupils in the School
of the Augustinians, when an officer entered and
read the sentence of condemnation passed upon him
by the council.

For a moment he remained silent; he then rose and
said, " You ought first to have shown me that I am
in error," and then he challenged his opponents to
refute his published opinions.

Receiving for reply that he must either submit to
silence or imprisonment, he said, " Then I appeal to
the King and the Parliament."

The Duke of Lancaster, becoming alarmed, hastened
to his old friend, and begged him—even ordered him
—to trouble himself no more about this matter.   But
the reformer was firm; it might cost him his life, but
he would abide by the truth.

As some time must elapse before the Parliament
again met, Wicliffe withdrew to Lutterworth; and
there, while quietly ministering to his flock, he, by
his voice in the pulpit, and by his pen, still further
diffused those sacred truths which he had drawn from
the Word of God.   He now published his tract,
entitled " The Wicket," an explanation in English of
the words, " This is my body "

In the summer of 1381 the people, oppressed by
their heavy burdens, and the severity of the tax-
collectors, rose in rebellion, and, led by Wat Tyler
and a dissolute priest named Ball, marched upon
London.   Strengthened by the lower orders of the
city, they burnt the magnificent palace of the Duke
of Lancaster in the Savoy, and seizing Sudbury the

Primate, then Chancellor of the kingdom, they beheaded him in the Tower. Other officers of State were also condemned to death. In a few days the insurrection was quelled, and its leaders, together with hundreds of their followers, executed.

The enemies of the Reformation endeavoured to lay the blame of this insurrection to the teaching of Wicliffe, and to cast opprobrium upon him and his cause in consequence. But the Gospel incites not to deeds of violence, and the sympathy of the insurrectionists with the mendicant friars—the avowed enemies of Wicliffe—is proof that he was not the one who led the people on to rebellion.

Immediately after the insurrection of Wat Tyler and his followers, Courtenay, the Bishop of London, was made Primate in the place of Sudbury. His translation to the primacy was secured by a bull from Pope Urban VI., and this increased his scrupulous submission to the pleasure of the papacy. He was a most zealous opponent of the reformer, and, as soon as the pall—the badge and insignia by which the Pope conveys to bishops the authority to act in his name—arrived, he convoked a synod to try the Rector of Lutterworth.

The court met on the 17th of May, 1382, in the hall of the Dominican Monastery, Blackfriars, London. It consisted of eight prelates, fourteen doctors, six bachelors of divinity, fifteen mendicant friars, and four monks. Truly an impartial assembly to try the Gospel doctor!

The members had just taken their seats, and were

proceeding to business, when an earthquake shook the city. The monastery trembled. The members of the court, much alarmed, turned to its president, and demanded an adjournment. It seemed as if the Divine displeasure rested upon their inquiry.

The Archbishop skilfully applied this incident to his own purpose. "Know you not," said he, "that the noxious vapours which catch fire in the bosom of the earth, and give rise to these phenomena which alarm you, lose all their force when they burst forth? Well, in like manner, by rejecting the wicked from our community, we shall put an end to the convulsions of the Church." The trial proceeded.

An officer of the court read out twenty-four propositions selected from the writings of the reformer. After the "good deliberation" of three days, it was agreed that ten of these were heretical, and the remainder erroneous. The sentence of this court was sent to the Bishop of London,—the metropolis being scarcely less infected by Wicliffe's doctrines than Oxford,—and to all his brethren, the suffragans of the diocese of Canterbury; and also to the Bishop of Lincoln, in whose diocese Lutterworth was situated; and it was accompanied by the commands of Courtenay, as "Primate of all England," that they should look to it that these pestiferous doctrines were not taught in their dioceses.

Another mandate was addressed to the Primate's Commissioner at Oxford, enjoining him to publish throughout the University the decisions of the synod, and commanding that all persons holding or main-

LUTTERWORTH CHURCH.

taining the errors specified, be holden in the strictest abhorrence under the penalty of the great anathema.

The University was, however, a hot-bed of heresy, and was but little inclined to carry out the commands of the Archbishop. Courtenay, therefore, carried his complaint to the young King, Richard II. "If we permit this heretic," said he, " to appeal continually to the passions of the people, our destruction is inevitable ; we must silence these Lollards."

Many circumstances at this time made it appear politic for the Crown to approach nearer to the Church. It was easy, therefore, for such a prelate as Courtenay to prevail. The King gave authority "to confine in the prisons of the State any who should maintain the condemned propositions."

A motion was carried through the House of Lords to this effect, but was not passed by the Commons. Although without the consent of the Commons it could not become law, an ordinance, dated 26th May, 1382, was placed on the statute-book substantially embodying its requirements.

A fierce persecution now commenced against the reformer and his followers. Lancaster, who upheld Wicliffe so long as the struggle was a political one, feared to follow him into the region of heresy. Some of his disciples forsook him ; enemies closed around ; but his trust was not in man, his hope was in God ; and, while persecution was being carried on against those who professed his tenets, and threatened to strike him down himself, he prepared to go yet another step forward.

Parliament re-assembled on the 19th of November, 1382. Wicliffe, who felt that he might be struck down at any moment, resolved that his countrymen should not be ignorant of the opinions for which he suffered. He, therefore, made haste to present his appeal to the King and the Parliament.

In this document he pointed out four grievances, and for each he demanded a very sweeping measure of reform. He first declared against the monastic orders, and pleaded for their abolition; secondly, he asserted that secular lords might lawfully and meritoriously, in many cases, take away temporal goods given to the Church; he next affirmed that even tithes and voluntary offerings should be withdrawn from priests who were guilty of great sins; and in the last he pleaded that the doctrine of the eucharist, as taught by Christ and His apostles, might also be taught openly in the churches.

This appeal made a great impression upon the Commons. They presented a petition to the King requiring that the persecuting statute, obtained by the Primate, might be disannulled, and declaring that it was not their intention that either they themselves or their successors should be further bound to the prelates than were their ancestors in former times. The King granted their request, and the statute was repealed.

Both the Parliament and Convocation were at this time assembled at Oxford. Baffled in the Parliament, Courtenay turned to Convocation. Here he could count upon having a more subservient court.

The clergy assembled were 'informed "that their business was to grant a subsidy to the Crown; and to remedy certain disorders which had too long disgraced the University, and were rapidly extending to the whole community, of whose spiritual safety they were the properly constituted guardians."

In this meeting the Archbishop had concentrated his whole strength. Six bishops, many doctors in divinity, and a host of inferior clergy, were there; the concourse being swelled by the dignitaries and youths of Oxford. Before this assembly Wicliffe was cited to appear.

Forty years had passed since he entered Oxford as a scholar; its halls had witnessed the toils of his youth and the labours of his manhood; but now it appeared to be turning against him.

He came now to be tried, perhaps condemned; and, if his judges were able, to be delivered to the civil power for punishment as a heretic. A solemn silence reigned as the reformer stood alone before his judges, calm and firm.

The indictment turned specially upon Transubstantiation. Did he affirm or deny that cardinal doctrine of the Church? Lancaster had advised him to submit in all doctrinal matters to the judgment of his order. But he was bound by his conscience and the Word of God, and he could not deny. Raising his venerable head, and looking with his clear, piercing eyes straight at Courtenay, he reproached the priests for disseminating error in order to sell their masses, and then, stopping, uttered these simple but energetic words, "The truth shall prevail."

"Having thus spoken," says D'Aubigné, he prepared to leave the court. His enemies dared not say a word; and like his Divine Master at Nazareth, he passed through the midst of them, and no man ventured to stop him."

Leaving Oxford, he retired once more to Lutterworth.

And is this all? Can reason do no more
Than bid me shun the deep and dread the shore?
Sweet moralist! afloat on life's rough sea,
The Christian has an art unknown to thee:
He holds no parley with unmanly fears;
Where Duty bids he confidently steers,
Faces a thousand dangers at her call,
And, trusting in his God, surmounts them all.

CHAPTER IX.

Conclusion.

"Henceforth there is laid up for me a crown of righteousness, which the Lord, the righteous Judge, shall give me at that day."—2 TIM. iv. 8.

ICLIFFE reached Lutterworth in safety. His remaining days were passed in peace, undisturbed by his enemies. Their enmity was unabated, but God in a marvellous manner protected His servant. The schism of the Popes, the political troubles of England, the favour with which the Duke of Lancaster still regarded him, all combined to form a rampart around the reformer.

"His very courage, in the hand of God, was his shield; for, while weaker men were apprehended and compelled to recant, Wicliffe, who would burn but not recant, was left at liberty." He himself expected nothing but imprisonment and death.

In his "Trialogus," written about this time, he said: "We have no need to go among the heathen in order to die a martyr's death; we have only to preach

persistently the law of Christ in the hearing of
Cæsar's prelates, and instantly we shall have a
flourishing martyrdom, if we hold out in faith and
patience."

In this work, Truth, Falsehood, and Wisdom were
personified, and between them they discussed all the
principal religious topics of the day. Truth proposed
questions, Falsehood raised objections, and Wisdom
declared sound doctrine.

As Wicliffe's weakness increased, he was assisted
in his pastoral duties by one of his followers, named
John Horn ; while another, named John Purvey,
became his constant attendant, his diligent co-
worker, and his confidential friend. Purvey wrote
out and collected many of the reformer's discourses,
which have in consequence been preserved, and a
few years after Wicliffe's death he revised his translation of the Bible.

During the two years which intervened between
his appearance at the Oxford Synod and his death,
Wicliffe continued zealously at work. Portions of
the Scriptures in the English language, tracts on
prayer, on the Catechism, on the doctrines of the
Church, on preaching, on pastoral work, on the life
and conversation which should characterise priests,—
all issued from the Rectory at Lutterworth.

It has generally been stated that, one day during
this period, while the reformer was quietly toiling
with his pen, he received a summons from the
Pontiff to appear at Rome ; and that while declining
on account of his age and infirmities, to obey the

command, he wrote a letter to Pope Urban VI. firmly upholding the truth of the doctrines he had taught. This story, however, seems, upon careful examination, to rest on no basis of authority, and Lechler states that "this alleged citation to Rome must be relegated to the category of groundless traditions."

In 1382 a crusade set forth from England to fight for the cause of Urban VI. against the supporters of the rival Pope, Clement VII. Every effort was made to induce as many as possible to join in this crusade, either personally or by donations. Indulgences were granted, available for both the living and the dead, to all who should assist; while those who opposed this sacred enterprise were anathematised.

Wicliffe viewed these proceedings with shame and displeasure. In the summer of 1383 he published a tract "Against the War of the Clergy," in which he severely condemned the crusade and all connected with it.

The end now drew near. Towards the close of 1382 the reformer had been stricken with paralysis, but from this he partially recovered. He was in his church at Lutterworth, in the midst of his beloved flock, on the last Sunday in 1384, engaged in the administration of the Sacrament of the Lord's Supper. As he was in the act of consecrating the bread and wine, he was again stricken with paralysis, and fell to the ground. His friends affectionately carried him from the church to the rectory, and laid him upon his bed. He continued speechless until the 31st of

December, when he was called up higher; his life and the year 1384 ending together.

His enemies saw in the circumstances of his death the terrible judgment of God, but his friends looked upon this as the glorious conclusion of a noble life. "None of its years, scarcely any of its days, were passed unprofitably on the bed of sickness. The moment his great work was finished, that moment the voice spake to him, which said, 'Come up hither!'"

> Then, with no throbs of fiery pain,
>   No cold gradation of decay,
> Death broke at once the vital chain
>   And freed his soul the nearest way.

Of the character and opinions of John Wicliffe we have space to say but little. He possessed that combination of opposite qualities which marks the great man. With a keenness that enabled him to follow all the intricacies and subtleties of scholastic argument, he united a temper eminently practical. He penetrated with intuitive insight to the root of all the evils that afflicted England, and with rare practical sagacity he devised and set in motion the true remedies for those evils. The evil he saw was ignorance, the remedy with which he sought to cure it was light. He therefore translated the Bible, and organised a body of pious earnest teachers to spread the truths of the Gospel throughout the land.

As a patriot, he strove to deliver his country from the tyranny of the papacy. He pointed out its true character, and by his influence he led the Parliament of England to resist the claims of Rome, and to assert the independence of the nation.

As a scholar, he was unquestionably the most extraordinary man of his age. He occupied the chair of theology in the first seminary of the kingdom, a fact proving his proficiency in the science of the schoolmen ; additional evidence of which is afforded by his writings, and also by the reluctant testimony of his enemies. " Not only his adherents, but even his opponents looked upon him as having no living equal in learning and scientific ability ; to all eyes he shone as a star of the first magnitude."

As a preacher he was earnest, devout, and faithful. His sermons which have been preserved are of two kinds, those written in Latin, preached before the university, and those written in English, preached to his congregation at Lutterworth and to assemblies of the common people elsewhere. These latter are free from the phraseology of the schools, and are full of intellectual strength, but plain in language, and fresh and vitalising in power.

Above all his other knowledge, Wicliffe possessed a profound acquaintance with the Scriptures. He studied the Bible, he venerated it as the Word of God. He held that it contained a perfect revelation of the Divine will; a full, plain, and infallible rule of both what man is to believe, and what he is to do. He fully received its truths into his heart and governed his actions by its teachings. Turning away from all human guides, he prayerfully and diligently searched the Scriptures to know the will of God, and then bowed to that will with the docility of a child.

Bowing himself to the authority of the Divine Word he endeavoured to get all men to submit to it. His great aim was to bring men back to the Bible. He exalted it as the one great authority before which all should bow, the law which infinitely exceeded all other laws, the book above all other books, for "other writings," he declared, " can have worth or authority only so far as their sentiment is derived from the Scriptures."

Of Wicliffe's personal piety there can be no doubt. It is true that scarcely any memorials of his private life remain, but his public history is an enduring monument of his personal Christianity. Tradition describes him as a most exemplary pastor, devoting a portion of each morning to relieving the needy, and consoling the aged, the sick, and the dying. In his manuscript for the order of priesthood, he states, "Good priests, who live well in purity of thought, speech, and deeds, and in good example to the people, who teach the law of God up to their knowledge, and labour fast, night and day to learn it better, and teach it openly and constantly, these are very prophets of God, and the spiritual lights of the world!" This was his ideal, and his writings and public actions prove that his life agreed thereto.

As an author he was most industrious. Soon after his death it was affirmed that his writings were as numerous as those of Augustine. Like his sermons, his works were written some in Latin, and others in

English. Notwithstanding all the efforts made to destroy them, large numbers are yet in existence. The libraries of the British Museum, of Trinity College, Dublin, the Bodleian Library at Oxford, the library at Lambeth Palace, the Imperial Library at Vienna, and others, are enriched by the writings of the reformer. His most important work was his translation of the Scriptures, but the "Poor Caitiff," a collection of tracts on practical Christianity, written in English for the instruction of the poorer people, and "The Wicket," before alluded to, became very popular, and produced a profound impression.

Of Wicliffe's doctrines we can give but a very brief summary. He denied the temporal power of the Pope, as well as his claim to be the spiritual head of the Church. He upheld the right of private judgment, when prayerfully and carefully exercised, in the interpretation of Scripture; and declared free remission of sins through the atonement of the Lord Jesus Christ. Sanctification by the aid of the Holy Spirit he taught in the following, as well as in other passages: "All our sufficiency is of God, through the mediation of Jesus Christ, thus of sinful and ungrateful men God maketh good men, and all the goodness in this cometh of God. Nor trouble we about the first cause, since God Himself is certainly the first cause."

While preaching a free salvation through a crucified Saviour he insisted on the necessity for self-denial and holiness, "Christ not compelling," said he, "but freely counselling every man to seek a perfect life, saith, 'Let him deny himself, and take up his cross and follow Me.' Let us then deny ourselves in whatever we have made ourselves by sin, and such as we are made by grace let us continue."

The belief in an intermediate state appears in some of the writings of the reformer, but he denounced with severity the representations that were made of suffering souls in purgatory, and the lucrative trade that was carried on by the priests " inventing new pains, horrible and shameful, to make men pay a great ransom."

The doctrine of the invocation of saints he opposed, and he condemned the worship of images. He held that " confession made to those who are true priests, and who understand the will of God, doth much good to sinful men, so long as contrition for past sins comes therewith "; but his parting advice on this subject was, " confess thyself to God, with constancy and contrition, and He may not fail, He will absolve thee."

The falseness of the doctrine of indulgences he freely exposed. " Prelates," said he, " foully deceive Christian men by their pretended indulgences or pardons and rob them wickedly of their money." Transubstantiation as taught by the Church of Rome, we have already seen, he declared to be contrary to the teaching of Scripture.

Wicliffe foretold that from the bosom of monkery would some day proceed the regeneration of the Church. " If the friars whom God condescends to teach shall be converted to the primitive religion of Christ," said he, " we shall see them abandoning their unbelief and returning freely, with or without the permission of anti-christ, to the religion of the Lord, and building up the Church as did St. Paul." Thus did his piercing glance discover at the distance of nearly a century and a-half, the young monk, Luther, in the Augustine convent at Erfurt, converted by the Epistle to the Romans, and returning to the spirit of St. Paul and the religion of Jesus Christ.

The Lollards, as the followers of Wicliffe were called, probably from their singing in a low or hushed voice, suffered cruel persecution after his death. Some were burnt, others imprisoned, till at last it seemed as though the leaven of the reformer had been eradicated from England, and that the morning star of the Reformation had shone in vain; but as the wind wafts the seed from one place to another, so the doctrines of John Wicliffe were wafted from Britain to the continent of Europe, and being carried into Bohemia by Jerome of Prague, they were embraced by John Huss, and afterwards took deep root and prepared the minds of the people for the great Reformation of the sixteenth century.

Thirty years had passed since the reformer's death, when the Council of Constance condemned a number of propositions which were said to have been extracted from his writings; and, as it appeared that he died an obstinate heretic, his memory was pronounced infamous, and it was decreed " that his body and bones should be taken from the ground and thrown away from the burial of any church, according to the canon laws and decrees ! "

In pursuance of this decree, a few years afterwards his grave at Lutterworth was opened, and his remains removed. These were then burnt, and the ashes cast into the adjoining brook named the "Swift," and Fuller, describing the scene, quaintly but truly says: "This brook conveyed them into Avon, the Avon into the Severn, the Severn into the narrow seas, they into the main ocean; and thus the ashes of Wicliffe were the emblem of his doctrine, which is now dispersed all the world over."

> As thou these ashes, little brook! will bear
> Into the Avon, Avon to the tide
> Of Severn, Severn to the narrow seas,
> Into main ocean they, this deed accursed,
> An emblem yields to friends and enemies,
> How the bold Teacher's doctrine, sanctified
> By truth, shall spread, throughout the world dispersed.

JOHN WICLIFFE SENDS HIS BIBLE TEACHERS OUT INTO THE WORLI